The Teller's Cage

The Teller's Cage

POEMS AND IMAGINARY MOVIES

BY

John Philip Drury

ABLE MUSE PRESS

Able Muse Press

www.ablemusepress.com

Printed in the United States of America

Names: Drury, John, 1950- author.
Title: The teller's cage : poems and imaginary movies / by John Philip Drury.
Description: San Jose, CA : Able Muse Press, 2024.
Identifiers: LCCN 2023003210 (print) | LCCN 2023003211 (ebook) | ISBN 9781773491394 (paperback) | ISBN 9781773491400 (ebook)
Subjects: LCGFT: Poetry.
Classification: LCC PS3554.R83 T45 2023 (print) | LCC PS3554.R83 (ebook) | DDC 811/.54--dc23/eng/20230127
LC record available at https://lccn.loc.gov/2023003210
LC ebook record available at https://lccn.loc.gov/2023003211

Cover image: *The Teller's Cage* by Mark Andres
Cover & book design by Alexander Pepple

John Philip Drury photo (on page 111) by Lisa A. Ventre

Able Muse Press is an imprint of *Able Muse*: A Review of Poetry, Prose & Art—at www.ablemuse.com

Able Muse Press
467 Saratoga Avenue #602
San Jose, CA 95129

And at home by the fire, whenever you look up, there I shall be—and whenever I look up, there will be you.

— Gabriel Oak's words to Bathsheba Everdene
in Thomas Hardy's *Far from the Madding Crowd*

Acknowledgments

Grateful acknowledgment is made to the editors of the following publications in which these poems, or earlier versions, first appeared:

Able Muse: "The Ruined Aristocrat"

The American Journal of Poetry: "Crossing Guard," "Curriculum Vitae," "Embarking," "Gossip," and "The Teller's Cage"

Ascent: "Chameleons" and "The Poet as a Seven-Year-Old Baseball Fan"

Contemporary Ghazals: "Ghazal of the Vaporetto"

Hampden-Sydney Poetry Review: "Executor" and "Things I Like about Frederick the Great"

The Hudson Review: "Rebecca in the Shadows"

Inertia: "Chaconne" and "Patricia Keene"

Iron Horse Literary Review: "The Civil War Goes On"

Literary Matters: "Flammable"

Live Encounters Poetry & Writing: "Arguing about Computers," "Daily Constitutional," "Library in a Dresser Drawer," "Listening to *A Love Supreme*," "Poised," "Recovering What's Lost," and "Streets Full of Water"

Main Street Rag: "Gaslight District" and "Social Networking"

Maryland Literary Review: "Crèche Scene with My Son" and "Horseback Riding"

Measure Review: "Autumn from a Passing Corolla" and "The Electric Guitarist"

New York Quarterly: "The Atheists of Junior High"

Nine Mile: "Chain Saw Blues," "Cincinnati Haiku," and "The Projectionist"

Passager: "Choosing a Reader"

Pine Row: "The Teller's Love Life"

Poet Lore: "New Song of the South"

The Poetry Porch (Sonnet Scroll): "Daughter of a Preacher Man," "Living in Monterey," and "Valentine for LaWanda"

Relief: A Journal of Art and Faith: "Beginning with a Line from Turgenev's *On the Eve*" and "Cherry Blossoms around the Tidal Basin"

River Styx: "E Pluribus"

Southern Poetry Review: "Windfall in Baltimore" (then titled "Chestnuts")

Valparaiso Poetry Review: "Going to a Ball Game with the Budapest String Quartet" and "Round Up"

Western Humanities Review: "Reverse Pindaric Ode for Olympic Athletes Who Don't Win Any Medals"

"Social Networking" was reprinted on *Verse Daily* (November 5, 2021). "The Electric Guitarist" was reprinted on the *Free State Review* /Galileo Press website (May 28, 2022).

I want to thank Jody Bolz, Brian Brodeur, Gregory Dowling, Alex Pepple, and the late Claudia Emerson for their help with some of these poems. Jordan Smith gave me many useful suggestions for revising "The Ruined Aristocrat." Nicholas Molbert compiled the words I drew at random (*wave, gossip, juice, look, emboss*) for a word-list exercise in a graduate seminar I taught on "The Sources of Poetry," helping me generate "Gossip," which turned into a rondeau. I also want to thank the other members of that class: Taylor Byas, Marianne Chan, Emily Rose Cole, Cara Dees, Lisa Low, Matthew Yeager, and Connor Yeck.

While I was on sabbatical from the University of Cincinnati, friends provided retreats where I worked on "The Ruined Aristocrat": *Little Pocket*, Susan Glassmeyer's "home away from home" in Empire, Michigan, and *Back of Beyond*, the chalet of Rick Cook, Owen Smith, and James Carter on a wooded hillside overlooking Gatlinburg, Tennessee, a vacation home destroyed in a wildfire on November 28, 2016, a month after my wife LaWanda and I stayed there. I'm grateful to Susan, Rick, Owen, and James for their generosity.

As always, I thank LaWanda Walters for her sharp critical eye, encouragement, and essential support.

Contents

The Teller's Cage

III

Trembling Scale

IV

To Go in the Dark

V

The Lexicon of Things That Morph

VI

The Teller's Cage

For me, a film is ninety-nine percent finished with the screenplay. Sometimes, I'd prefer not to have to shoot it. You conceive the film you want and after that everything goes to pieces. The actors you had in mind are not available, you can't get a proper cast. I dream of an I.B.M. machine in which I'd insert the screenplay at one end and the film would emerge at the other end, completed, and in color. . . .

— Alfred Hitchcock

Lord when I look at lovely things which pass,
    Under old trees the shadow of young leaves
Dancing to please the wind along the grass,
    Or the gold stillness of the August sun on the August sheaves;
Can I believe there is a heavenlier world than this?

— Charlotte Mew, "In the Fields"

The Teller's Cage

I

Get on Board, Little Children

The Poet as a Seven-Year-Old Baseball Fan

In an old photo, I'm crouching by a blackboard,
wearing pajamas, pointing at a lineup
in chalk. And batting fourth, bold-lettered, starred,
appears a forgotten player, Al Pilarcik.
I can't recall his team or his position.
He was a nobody, but his name enchanted,
the lilting, heft, and click of syllables.
More than the game itself, I loved the names,
murmuring *Mickey Mantle, Minnie Minoso,*
male counterparts to Marilyn Monroe.

Somehow, I always got the lessons wrong.
A flip-book showing how to swing a bat
instructed me in how to make a movie.
In a real batter's box, I flinched at pitches,
swung wildly, defensively, my glasses fogged
and falling down my nose. Fear spoiled the sport.
Under a canopy of sycamores
by the Tred Avon River, I tossed a ball
up through the leaves and crooned *Duke Maas, Duke Maas,*
loving the double "a"—and *Gil McDougald.*

But pure sound and the euphony of names
gave way to facts—McDougald lined a fastball
right in the eye of Herb Score, pitcher whose name
I also loved to say, and toppled him,
ruining his career as he writhed on the mound.
I could identify with pain like that.

Beauty could find itself in contemplation
of things that hurt, like baseballs hurled and insults
erupting from the opposition's bench
and faces turned away on your own team.

Remembering embarrassment is to name it,
and names are lovely, tokens of breath, dark roses
that burst in fragrance you can't help but smell,
even in absence, in the mind alone.
Forget statistics. Names are what endure:
Pindar, Patroclus, Atalanta, Chronos.

Going to a Ball Game with the Budapest String Quartet

I went along as company for Mark,
my friend from school, whose father was the cellist.
The Senators were playing Kansas City,
bad teams that fought to dodge last place, a bad
introduction for new fans, the quartet
lifting and quaffing jumbo cups of beer.
The day was sunny, early spring, the crowd
buzzing between the catcalls and the cheers,
and I was serving as interpreter
who could explain runs, hits, foul balls, and strikeouts.

The game's absurdity first made them frown,
as though they smelled something bad, or got a blast
of rock and roll, but soon they joked in Russian,
exploding into laughter, almost dancing
in their hard seats, and I could picture them
moving together in hilarity
at Beethoven's epic jesting, still an ensemble
in the scherzo of a noisy stadium.

Chameleons

1.

They can't match backgrounds, really, but we need
the metaphor. Mom bought one at the circus
when I was eight years old. She kept the string
around its neck and leashed it to a curtain,
secured by a safety pin. I don't recall
naming the thing, and when we moved away
my mother gave it to a science teacher
at Cambridge Junior High. But when I think
of our lost cottage on the Eastern Shore
of Maryland, the small chameleon's there,
alive in the color wheel of memory,
refusing to change, as I could not refuse
losing my accent, trying to blend in
and be invisible. His claws grip fabric,
motionless and dark on the sunlit drape.

2.

Checking facts, I found that I was wrong
to think the lizard clutching our bark-cloth folds
was a chameleon, the only term
my mother ever flaunted in her stories.
The vendors at the circus called them "bugs,"
but online research proved our curtain pet
was really an *anole* (rhymes with *cannoli*):
a *dactyloid*, clinger to surfaces,
capable of changing from green to brown
because of stress, aggression, social greetings,
but not, apparently, for camouflage.

The chords of accuracy are dissonant.
Errata raise objections in the margins,
in after-the-fact disclaimers, but also in
the palinode, which Stesichorus used,
retracting what the rhapsodes sang of Helen:
it wasn't true; she never sailed to Troy.

I wonder, now, how much my mom embellished,
turning distortions to anecdotal beauty.
We bought a tiny lizard at the circus
and tethered it to drapery in our house.
But when we left town, did a science teacher
keep it in a terrarium in his lab?
Or did my mother set it loose outside?
Or flush it? Our house was gone, and so were we,
clinging to metaphor that bruised the truth
and getting facts wrong. But the story stays.
We're still chameleons who can't help changing.

Horseback Riding

I was the only boy in fifth grade
in love with horses, reading *Black Stallion* books,
doodling Appaloosas and palominos.

Late fall, indulging my equestrian dreams,
my mother drove her partner Carolyn
and me to a fancy dude ranch in Virginia.

The pillared mansion disappointed me,
more Civil War than Wild West, and I hated
the archery range, its targets on hay bales.

Yet I recall the joy of smelling hay
and horse manure, picking a mount to ride
but startled at how big he really was

and how my fantasies misled me, feeling
panic in the saddle when the gelding
bolted to a canter and I bounced,

clutching the pommel, until our guide rode up
and took the reins and calmed the frightened horse,
her words melodic: *There, it's all right, there.*

Round Up

We rode our bikes to the amusement park
built by a trolley company. Glen Echo
blessed our summers, especially in the dark
when strings of white lights emphasized art deco
curves and lines, cool breeze rising like high tide.
Done with the rickety roller coaster, we ran
downhill to the Round Up, our favorite ride,
and stood in cages as it rose and spun.

An illustration of centrifugal force,
the ride gave physics lessons with the thrill
of blast-off pressure on our chests. Of course,
only the back wall's metal mesh could quell
the body's impetus to fly away—
wild boys, bewildered, tearing off each day.

The Atheists of Junior High

clobbered and dazed me dumb, their confidence
as titillating as a sip of wine.
Not that I'd had much. My experience
was limited to port, kneeling in line

at the communion railing in our church.
All girls, they awed me, exulting in disbelief,
as fiery as my camp counselor's torch
that lit a nighttime hike along a bluff.

My camp had daily chapel. And I used
to sing in choirs, adoring hymns and prayers.
But I was fascinated and seduced
by the cool talk of Janice and of Clare,

who stirred me up, my agitated soul,
making their godlessness divine in school.

Cherry Blossoms around the Tidal Basin

White blossoms, dropping
white shadows on the dark drive
around the white dome.

Back in 1968: class ring I lost playing baseball at dusk.

Families picnic
near shrines, under *sakura*—
Kyoto. DC.

White kids made sandwiches, filling boxes for King's *Poor People's Campaign*.

Muddy shantytown
of Resurrection City—
canned goods on pallets.

Dark under trees along the Mall, hammers bashed wood struts to hold up tarps.

Because of riots
our prom moved to the suburbs—
clubhouse on golf course.

Spring of assassinations. Teriyaki sauce on my cummerbund.

The night of the prom
we parked by the rotunda—
blossoms lit the car.

Did the moon shimmy on the water? I don't remember. Did we dance?

Jefferson watched us
not kissing in my mom's car,
quiet in the glow.

Never ready for the festival, they're late bloomers, slow to wake up.

Floral commotion
then a silence of bare limbs—
flowers without fruit.

New Song of the South

Just before dark, I like to walk my dog
along a hilly, curving, shadowy street,
ash trees with yellow *x*'s on the trunks
and paper birches, their ragged flaps of bark.
The thicket of leafy darkness brings me back
to a picture book of Uncle Remus stories,
its cartoon illustrations from Disney's film,
long banned from circulation. *Zip-a-Dee-Doo-Dah*,
I sang along, happy and unenlightened,
too young to know I was indulging in
nostalgia for the antebellum South.

Too young for other literature, I found
my epic in these stories: moon in the millpond,
cypress of crows, tar baby on a log.
But even then, I loathed the live-action frame,
the little white kids and the kindly slave,
white-haired, smoking a pipe, happy to sit
in his rough cabin, entertaining them.
Where were his own grandchildren? Down the river,
sold at auction? Or did they steal away,
Br'er Rabbit diving into the briar patch,
safe house for transit to the starry North?

Here's how to resurrect the film, redeem it:
keep the cartoons, those spirituals of outsmarting
fat bears and foxes in their confederacy
of ignorance and greed, but change the frame
to celebrate the owners of the stories,
not cavaliers whose property was human.

Make Remus wily, wild to get away,
imparting lore beside the blazing fireplace
to rapt black faces, his own family.

It's after midnight on a moonless night.
A shadow fills the doorframe, not the master
and not the straw boss, gripping a buggy whip,
but a Black woman, head scarf and slouch hat,
Harriet Tubman, pistol in her hand
"Come on, now, hurry. Get up and follow me."

And then the cabin's bare. The woods embrace
escapees who have entered. Like a burrow,
the Underground Railroad hides them from pursuit.
There's nothing but a flicker in the dark:
a cottontail that pauses on a footpath
before he merges into underbrush.

Another sunrise bares the cotton fields.
And here comes Joel Chandler Harris, traipsing
along the brickwork of the garden path,
conversing with a white-haired, red-faced colonel:
"Hear tell he was a right good storyteller.
Well, never mind, there's always the next plantation."

Then let the rescued movie end with song—
Paul Robeson, his bass voice booming out,
"Get on board, little children, get on board"—
and one farewell cartoon. Br'er Rabbit, born
in Africa, stowaway on the Middle Passage,
leans back against a live oak, feigning sleep,
trickster who's figuring out his next escape.

II

A War That's Secretive and Personal

Reverse Pindaric Ode for Olympic Athletes Who Don't Win Any Medals

Crushed runners, immobile,
kneeling on cinders, flat
on the track's grassy verge,
beyond mere weeping, wail
like the women of Troy,
the medal stand beyond
the range of their sprinting,
medals glinting like lights
of a cruise ship sailing
off from the passenger
thrown overboard, treading
water in the dark sea.

In practice, in dreams, it never went like this,
maybe a side stitch, pulled muscle, ankle sprain,
never anything beyond the balm of hope.
In ancient Greece, it would be far worse, no way
to go back home at all, injured or not, if
you failed to win. No silver. No bronze. No wreath
or prizes, no Pindar or big production
in your honor, just a dusty or muddy
road in the opposite direction from home.

You counted on making a name for yourself.
In defeat, all you expected was to be
forgotten, nothing more than wind that lunges
through a stadium, over a mountain range,
a force without embodiment, although winds
have names, of course: Föhn, mistral, Santa Ana,
simoom, Alberta Clipper, and sirocco,
even "Maria" in the musical. But
no name in lights for you, accomplished loser.

> You could just die, but death
> rejects you too and says,
> "Go back, you flop, you dud,
> you failure, you phony!
> Not much of a runner,
> so start walking. In fact,
> you can still run, can't you,
> you faker. Maybe not
> fast enough, far enough,
> but Point A to Point B
> is surely doable.
> Nike says, 'Just do it.'"

But there it is, there *she* is, Nike, goddess
of victory, more than a logo that's like
a boomerang, curling comet tail, hooked moon,
more than some corporation or running shoe.
You can still hobble off, the ankle will heal
(or not), and maybe you'll limp and look gimpy,
bystanders poking fun or sympathizing,
and victory come, if at all, in private
benedictions upon your bowed head, hurt heart.

If you're empty now, you can't get emptier,
and anything might refill your begging bowl:
snow falling outside the café's curved window
as you sip tea and rest your feet in new boots,
as you use the bottom of a pool's deep end
to push upward, exploding into the wind
that blows just hard enough to remind you how
Keats's "life of sensations" is really what
we've got, the dolphin's nudge that buoys us.

Curriculum Vitae

After Lisel Mueller

1) I was born on the banks of a tidal river.

2) My father, an Army reservist,
was called up for Korea but never got there, lucky
to come down with pneumonia.

3) School was a haven of sliced apples
and carrot sticks, a principal who didn't punish
lawbreakers who talked out of turn.

4) Third grade was joyful in discoveries, hellish
in ruptures: my father leaving, my mother spurning
her rich uncle's marriage proposal,
another mother joining us, the three of us
moving to Austin, where cowboys
still rode the range and sang in their saddles.

5) We never got to Texas.

6) We settled back home in our free state:
two women who called themselves cousins
so they could rent an apartment with their boy.

7) School made me shy, gave me tics, made me blink
one eye in reply to the other's blinking.

8) I dreaded standing in front of class,
speaking aloud, but I wrote a poem
about Spartans and Athenians, and after I read it,
the whole class applauded.

9) The poem was terrible, but it rhymed.

10) When I was thirteen, I wanted to go downtown
to the March on Washington, but my mother said no,
and I was a good boy. But I should have disobeyed.
And she should have gone with me, sharing that dream.

11) Skipping classes in college, I lost
my draft deferment. But I chose to enlist,
joining the Army to evade combat.

12) Marriage was difficult for my mother, and so
it was difficult for me. Years of trial, years of error.

13) When her partner, her secret wife, died, my mother
was having her hair done. The doctor said, *They leave
when they're ready. If they don't want you there,
they'll wait until you're gone.*

14) When my mother died, years later, I was there.
Hearing is the last thing to go, the nurse said,
so I talked to someone whose eyes remained closed,
playing arias and big-band music, recounting
the choices and joys of her life.

15) Now I live with my third wife, my last wife,
in a room we call our treehouse, in a house
that's tilting back toward a ravine.

16) Our screen porch borders an ocean of foliage.

17) The world turned upside down, we hold on to each other.

18) "The World Turned Upside Down" was the tune
Cornwallis's band played when he surrendered at Yorktown.

19) We don't surrender.

E Pluribus

One of the people loitering in the sad
sack of my body wants to murder you.
One is dying to beguile you into bed.
One wants to laze on the screen porch and view

the ghost ship of a fallen ash tree. One
scurries through neighbors' yards and garden plots,
trying to catch a greyhound on the run
before his rush at fluttering leaves or cats

propels him into traffic. I am legion,
but who isn't? It's a word for *moody*,
how Pollyanna merges with curmudgeon,
the schizophrenia we all embody.

I vote for you each day, my love, the count
unanimous in this one-man parliament.

Social Networking

In memory of Ray Bradbury

Facebook, for me, is not much fun,
as public as a nudist colony
      where I have nothing on,
like a bad dream in which onlookers see

    my tongue-tied shyness magnified.
Exposure makes me blush. What can I do?
      Strike back like Billy Budd?
Perch like a bird that's silent on a bough?

    Each naked sinner wears a mask
in a surrealist Last Judgment scene:
      flamingo plume or tusk
put on so profile photographs will stun.

    Fear of a booing crowd or fear
that no one gathers in this stadium
      makes me want to go where
Innisfree supplants Byzantium.

    Thank goodness, none of it's in print.
What floats upon the screen's ephemeral,
      easy to circumvent
by power outages, decline and fall.

    Thank goodness, Facebook's not a book
and no one's going to venture to the woods,
      taking a daily walk
to learn by heart the pulsing of its words.

Daily Constitutional

Now you can see, my son, how ludicrous
  And brief are all the goods in Fortune's ken,
Which humankind contend for. . . .
    — Dante, Inferno, *Canto VII (translated by Robert Pinsky)*

"If I can't take it with me, I'm not going,"
my aunt declared. She went, though, went alone
down isolated roads, darkened by clouds,
barefoot as Saint Francis but without
the holiness and good heart, searching for
a private beach, a gated community
excluding Blacks, Jews, gays, the lower classes,
searching for another wealthy husband.

She thought that purchasing a burial plot
in the county's swankiest graveyard guaranteed
she'd lounge in peace, but now she's on the move,
hobbling in circles, she who wouldn't ride
in anything that wasn't a Cadillac,
"nothing but the best." When I see her there,
I feel a twinge of pity, remembering
small kindnesses—a day at Frontier Town,
lunch on the porch with soft-crab sandwiches—
but think of Lady Luck and how she turns
the rich to wretched, how my aunt will get
not jewelry but the exercise she needs,
her circumambulation that is endless.

Chain Saw Blues

The building inspector said, "You need a chain saw."
> *Magnolia in full leaf about to come down*

Too many trash trees, so I need a chain saw.
> *Planted years back on the White House lawn*

I need to slash through laziness, my main flaw.
> *General Jackson had just come to town*

The safest power tool inflicts pain raw.
> *President Jackson craved whiffs of home*

Buzzing and shaking, it chafes my pain raw.
> *Black men, his slaves, dug in the loam*

But weeding the tangled mess lets my brain thaw.
> *Planting a sapling in the new Rome*

In the fun house, the boy said, "That's not a *real* chain saw."
> *Trees are temporary, but so is a president*

The boy, my stepson, gave me a new chain saw.
> *We'll blast the creepers that leave the truth bent*

Now I'll cut and clear for the sake of plain law.
> *Soon, Dante will report where the boss man's been sent*

Things I Like about Frederick the Great

1.
Not his tactics, his military prowess,
but dogs he brought along on his campaigns,
Italian greyhounds, sleeping in his tent.
Examining his portrait, I can see
the bulging bug-eyes that his dogs would have.
He called them his "marquises de Pompadour."

2.
When he was crown prince, still a teenager,
he tried to flee from Prussia—meaning his father—
but someone tattled, soldiers imprisoned him
along with friend and coconspirator
Hans von Katte, junior officer.
His father made him watch from a palace window
as an executioner beheaded Hans
with one sword stroke. The royal court agreed
the boys' attachment must have been romantic.

3.
He played the flute, composed sonatas, hired
a son of Bach and gave the father a string
of twenty notes on which to improvise
a six-part fugue, the Musical Offering—
a sinuous, haunting, booby-trapped labyrinth.

4.

Though Nazis claimed him as their hero, made
an epic movie when the war went badly,
they wouldn't let the King of Prussia rest
beside his dogs in the garden of Sanssouci
but moved his coffin constantly, from bunker
to bunker. But the king was never theirs,
enthusiast of the Enlightenment,
friend of Voltaire, who preferred philosophy
and music to warmongering—though he
was virtuoso of mass slaughter, too,
master of planning the oblique attack—
a linguist of half a dozen languages,
including Hebrew, who tolerated Jews
because he found them useful and because
he "never persecuted anyone,"
anti-Machiavellian, a *Mensch*,
a German leader who was not a monster,
loved men and making music and his greyhounds
by whom he rests now, in his royal garden,
not buried there until two centuries
of wandering had passed: a boy's wish
to join his pet dogs in the underworld.

The Civil War Goes On

In memory of Robert Altman

They haven't bathed since 1863—
Rebel and Union reenactors massed
near Gettysburg to mimic history,
calling themselves hardcore, eating hardtack,
pouring powder and blanks down musket barrels,
jamming ramrods, attaching percussion caps
to metal nipples that hammers strike for sparks.
They'd like a do-over, but there's a script
to follow, orders from dead generals.

They're in some pasture, not the battlefield
itself, too holy, packed with monuments.
It looks like county fairgrounds, where the land
has sprouted shooting galleries and rides.
No landmarks here. No Cemetery Ridge.
No Devil's Den or Little Round Top. Nothing
but a wide, rolling field that's suitable
for Pickett's Charge. Rebels look optimistic.
They came in minivans and pickup trucks
and pitched their realistic, smelly tents,
a bivouac of impersonators, women
in gingham dresses mending uniforms,
a sergeant yawning in a union suit
as red as blood that none of them will spill
except by accident. There's General Lee!
He circulates on Traveller, cheers the troops.
Confederates serving in the Stonewall Brigade

are southern, but their home's Ontario.
They're sweating by a campfire they've ignited
the old way, flint-and-steel or friction matches.
The morning's hot. The weather will be brutal
today, the anniversary of the battle.

Some girls are serving in the infantry.
The men did not say farewell to their sweethearts,
as in a Currier and Ives engraving,
but brought them here. And after "Taps," some tents
are rollicking with sex and shots of bourbon,
girlfriends and wives who have to reenact
the roles of General Hooker's "public women."
Others, though, disapprove and mind their children,
peeking under tent flaps to request
Please keep it down. We'd like to get some sleep.

Some of the Northern troops are integrated,
and every temporary soldier knows
the works of Shelby Foote and how to load
a musket with a Minié ball, attach
a bayonet, and march along dirt roads.
Friends tell jokes. But nobody can tell
an enemy by uniform alone.
It's always brother versus brother, always
Cain and Abel, fighting over rights
and property—not slaves, this time, but *Hey!*
That woman there you're trying to get drunk,
buddy, is mine, you butt-faced motherfucker.

Artillery is firing thunderous blanks,
volleying, gray lines and blue batteries,
companies marching toward objectives, hill
or tree line, bugles calling, some troops singing,
women watching through binoculars,
cavalry charging by, their sabers raised.
When shots go off, some soldiers fall and die—
how strange to drive so far and die so fast.
Where's the fake blood? How long must they play dead?
Then there's another sound. A siren blares.
An ambulance is racing across the fray
to aid a corporal who has just passed out.
The heat has started claiming casualties.
There's General Lee! He finds a handkerchief,
lifts up his hat (troops cheer, *Huzzah, Marse Robert!*),
wiping off sweat and wanting a mint julep.
Troops are wheeling, double-timing, charging
the enemy positions, falling on cue
and acting dead. And then it starts to rain.
Troops panic. It's a rout! Back to their camps
and vans they scurry, slipping in sudden mud,
canteens clanking, public address announcer
pleading for calm, for units to assemble.
It's what they call a general retreat.
No one has won. But someone's sprinting back,
splashing through puddles to the battlefield—
a body's lying motionless in mud.
Turned over, it's an infantry commander,
and he's not faking it, his guts blown open.
Real ammunition. Someone's loaded musket
has imitated war in all its glory.

At this point, though, the film is not half over.
Detectives mass, cordoning off the crime scene,
and everyone must reenact what happened,
first in interrogations—witnesses
in soggy uniforms—and then in flashbacks:
fights in basement rec rooms, sex in motels,
guns bought at swap meets, truck-stop parking lots,
the undertow of silent threats at parties.
A friend or enemy could have fired the shot,
following orders of a cheating spouse
or acting on his own initiative,
punishing the wicked, prosecuting
a war that's secretive and personal.
And maybe someone's caught, and maybe not,
rain falling through the smoke of discharged weapons,
even though all but one round have been blanks.

Mud, blood, smoke, rain. The civil war goes on
throughout the turning, turbulent republic,
with muted feuds and open bouts of loathing
in split communities, as well as here
in Pennsylvania, where the forecast's sunny
for tomorrow, Independence Day.

III

Trembling Scale

Rebecca in the Shadows

My daughter stretches out, half sunken in leaves,
the backyard's plush quilt of dark, jagged fragments.
The princess on her mattress, she feels nothing
alien beneath her, spreading her arms
to forge an angel's imprint in the fall.

I'm spying from the kitchen. She couldn't hear me
if I called through storm windows that won't open
or rapped the double pane. She's taking in
woodpeckers overhead, squirrels dropping acorns,
a cardinal chanting on a basketball hoop.
She grows still, motionless in mottled light,
looking above her at the patchwork sky
that shimmers like a dome enclosing her.

The tree house she won't play in adds its shadow
to the shifty camouflage of fading daylight.
Now I can't find her, so I have to look
harder for anything that moves in near darkness:
branch an opossum climbs, grass the wind ruffles.
If I go outside, she might be gone already.

Crèche Scene with My Son

No one would want that clinic on their lawn,
delivery room aglow in fluorescent light
where, since it belonged to a university,
each specialist had students who observed
the half-successful epidural drip.

The monitors that checked his vital signs
alarmed the nurses, who believed he might
be starved for air. They started agitating
to prep his mother for a cesarean,
but no, the wires had simply come unstuck.

The obstetrician, really just an intern
with pudgy fingers, washed his hands but froze
when it came time to deliver, so a nurse
waylaid a doctor passing in the hallway,
a surgeon from Algeria, tall and balding,
who stepped in, sat down, and shouted, "Push, push!"
unclogging what had stalled. The intern, still
in cap and mask, retreated to the wall,
deliverer of nothing, dazed by panic.

Two dozen medical professionals
crowded the bed, gawked at the baby Eric
who slid out like a football, though a nurse
still snipped to make a bigger opening,
giving her student the chance to sew it back.

They let me cut the cord. He had turned blue,
his scores low, but I gazed to memorize
his face and bare scalp. That was a good thing,
because when he was in intensive care,
a bossy nurse tried to hand me a baby
with full, dark, glossy hair. "That's not my son!"
I told her, but I had to plead until
she checked his name tag on the plastic bracelet.

He wasn't baptized, wasn't circumcised,
going naked into the secular world
without the primal memory of faces
crowding his crib to glimpse nativity,
seminar room of angels taking notes
and magi who left nothing when they left,
making their rounds, wearing their stethoscopes
like silver medals dangling over scrubs.

Windfall in Baltimore

For Vicki Metaxas, my ex-wife

On one of our hour-long walks
to run errands, we stumbled
on a windfall of chestnuts
beside Druid Hill Park,
some in the roadway, crushed
on macadam. At first
the shadows of leaves
camouflaged the harvest,
the welcome debris. Then wind
rose up, lifting the branches.

Stooping and turning, I saw
the brushed coats
of thoroughbreds, charred husks
in a pushcart, the varnished
ripples on a violin,
sunshine blotted white
on the grain. As we filled
our pockets, you recalled
roasting them on a campfire,
betting whose would pop first,
bursting into spices. All the while,
chestnuts fell as we bent and pivoted
and felt the light grow dimmer.

I remembered a driftwood sculpture.
Out of gnarled timber
a crescent emerged—
a nude torso, the polished grain
swirling at the nipples.
Beneath fluttering leaves,
I stopped to watch you
bending over our find, a crevice
of light on your body.
Hiking the long way back—
pockets crammed, kerchiefs
loaded with clicking—we heard
the source of castanets.

Back home on Charles Street,
we poured them on a table
and skimmed through recipes
for garnishes and forcemeats:
Cut a gash in the flat side.
Add marjoram, thyme, savory.
As water started boiling
I pulled down the tree book
and leafed until I found—
not chestnuts at all!
A blight. Whatever we'd gathered
tumbled and split in the boiling pot.

You said, "They *look* like chestnuts.
Sure they're chestnuts. Just you wait."
Cooked up, they were different:
boiled yellow nutmeat, bitter and mealy.
"So what are they anyway?"
We settled on sweet buckeye,
whose ground-up seeds "make paste
that repels all insects."
Rather than drop the rest
down the incinerator chute,
we kept them for a centerpiece.

Heaped in a bowl, they gave
the feel of depth:
a robber's cache, a basin
to dip our hands in.
I'd like to scoop up
a fistful now, that deep shade
of fire—to chance
upon it again each morning.

I would not discard—
along with useless fruit—
the swaying of branches
and your chestnut hair, the dipping
of our bodies as we gathered
what we couldn't ingest.
Though love recedes deeper each year
in the flickering shade,
the love poem remains.

Valentine for LaWanda

I fancied you the first night that we met,
guests at a party. I walked you to your car,
dying to ask you out for coffee, but
we weren't alone. Another bachelor
escorted both of us and foiled my hopes,
thwarting my shy desire to meet with you.
Another Southerner—but more a Snopes,
no gentleman—he spoiled our rendezvous.

That interference cost us many years.
Still, you were married then, though separated,
so we were forced to take the long way here,
friends first. But I regret how long I waited
to make a move and risk unwillingness.
It kills me that you would have answered, "Yes."

Listening to *A Love Supreme*

After John Coltrane

So long, so deep
a rush of droplets beside the moving loom
of the waterfall, oh, my love,
your Volvo speeding, that safe car swerving
and escaping
from first marriage, a house
built by a termite inspector
who battered you, roughed up your skull
and brain, but couldn't demolish
your gift for words, the art
he pretended to make,
and now I follow your progress—*so long,*
so deep—from redwoods to desert,
charting where I lived in your time of distress,
unaware
of our convergence to come,
years later, as I walked uphill
to the refugee camp
where I passed out questionnaires
to others who had fled,
as I too was fleeing, undercover
in a foreign country, waiting
for love, oh, my love, for you.

Poised

on top of a ravine, our Rose Hill haven,
century-old House of Usher, sanctuary
at risk, we keep a balance that's temporary
yet lasting—John Glenn's capsule, Friendship 7,
ready to plunge, unshielded, from airless heaven
back to the once-safe atmosphere that's fiery
enough to burn and devour his spacecraft, airy
furnace that's not damnation, just an oven.

Yet I skipped school, attended his parade,
and now take hope in coming through—while hung
teetering atop a stopped Ferris wheel
that's our existence here, a trembling scale
which feels like stillness, rest within a song
whose resonance rings the marriage we have made.

Flammable

The heart's torch
could kindle a thicket,
cruising the ridgeline
after midnight, like a car
with a broken headlight.
I watch it seething
beside a dark pond
where a woman swims laps
and emerges, picking up
her beach towel
and wrapping it tightly
around her torso. It's not
eternal, but its oils
burn so slowly
and its rags are packed
so thickly around its tip
the flame can't help
gulping cool air.
It wriggles and soars,
a story below
a set of drawn blinds.
The neighbor who can't sleep
wonders if it's meant
for her. She sits
at her window, sips tea,
and watches until the torch
slips away down the alley
beyond shut garages,
sputtering under the tinder
of dangling branches.

Patricia Keene

Each fall, the architecture school requires
all of its first-year students to erect
shelters on the slope beside the classrooms
and studios. They have a list of what
materials they are allowed to use:
cardboard instead of patterned cinder blocks,
scraps they can scavenge, anything like driftwood.
The problem is the site, which isn't level.
Weather is unpredictable, and they
must spend one night in their make-shift abodes.
Ambition counts. Refrigerator boxes
might do for derelicts but not for builders.
No shanty town. They try to emulate
their heroes whose designs are close at hand:
Frank Gehry, Peter Eisenman, Michael Graves,
especially Zaha Hadid. Patricia loves
her center for contemporary art.

She's found some green, translucent plastic sheets
for windows, fits them into openings
of trapezoids and parallelograms.
Diagonals play against the jutting ledges
for sleeping and for study. She even plants
a garden on the roof, with drainage channels:
Wind in the Willows meets Frank Lloyd Wright.

Everyone's busy building on the hillside,
but then she notices a man who's browsing,
inspecting their work, examining designs:
a homeless wanderer the students call
the Fuzzy Man, handsome enough to play
James Bond or Shaft (he could be black or white),
a stubbly beard, wild hair that looks like graphite.
Sometimes he pauses in his peregrinations
to open up a battered pocket notebook
and sketch—who knows what?—something that he's noticed.

Later that night, when everyone's retired,
experiencing their interiors,
she's reading by a battery-powered lantern
when there's a tapping on the cardboard door
and a voice says, "Knock, knock." Oh, no, she thinks,
some joker wants to hear her say, "Who's there?"
And so she opens up the door and sees
the Fuzzy Man. She feels hairs rise on her neck.
"I've brought you coffee for the night, decaf,
but flavored so it's like an opera cream."
She doesn't want to let him in but does,
and he sits down, cross-legged, on a blanket.
"Thank you," he says, "not everyone I meet
reciprocates. I won't stay long but like
the house you've built here. See? I've even sketched it.
Here, you keep it. No, it's yours. I'll go now."
He leaves, and what was that about, she wonders,
holding the pocket-notebook sheet ripped out.
It's really pretty good, she thinks, and smiles,
happy to savor coffee he provided.

Next morning, sunlight makes the whole room green.
When she emerges, though, there's cactus, sand,
a gleaming emerald city in the desert.
Ohio's been transformed to Arizona.
And she's dolled up, not wearing a plaid shirt
and overalls with speckles of white paint.
She gazes up at arches, cantilevers,
glass tinted green, a rooftop hanging garden,
walls with paintings on a swirl of tiles.
She realizes these are her designs,
except the murals. She starts walking, stunned.
When she looks back, the house she built is just
a stack of cardboard and green plastic sheets,
ready to be recycled the next day.

She soon discovers she's acquired a husband,
Rex Derringer, "No, call me Doctor, please,"
a man with law and medical degrees
who fools around with interns and assistants,
women and men, it doesn't matter which,
as long as he's on top and everyone's cool
and hip enough to treat it casually.

She's taken on a girlfriend, Mattie Dawson,
a painter who's been her collaborator
on houses, public buildings, a museum.
The work of Jennifer Bartlett comes to mind,
and that's seductive in itself, she thinks.

Everyone seems okay with this arrangement,
but Rex is ready to explode. He's not
on top. Mad logic is his only method.
Someone has got to vanish. Who will go?

One night, Patricia sees the Fuzzy Man
dressed in a stylish suit. He sips a cocktail.
"Help me get back," she pleads, "what do I do?"
"You don't. This is the life you have designed.
Forces at work are structural. Think physics."
He wasn't homeless now, apparently,
and really wasn't much help as a genie.
She'd made a leap, and now she couldn't leave.
One vote, and no one gets another chance,
but there are other opportunities
for choice, to go with Mattie and refuse
to murder or be murdered. She consults
her drafting table and begins designing.

IV

To Go in the Dark

The Projectionist

In memory of Liam Rector

We were good friends when we were desperate,
shirking work, writing letters on the job,
"cheating our employer," as Frost would say.
You came back to Baltimore and took me drinking,
and I got drunk enough, at the Cat's Eye,
to change my mind about my future plans,
declining a fellowship, relinquishing
a funky apartment and a doctorate.
You lured me to an office in New York,
a minor job in arts administration
that I regretted. But I did enjoy
going out to lunch together there—
Papaya King or the hot, smoky joint
that advertised itself as "Home of the Flameburger,"
no diet for your undiagnosed conditions.

You had another first name when we met,
but Liam did what Ron could not have done,
your way to "make it new." I never told you
I tried to change my name when I was serving
as an interrogator in the Army,
living in Zirndorf, posing as a civilian,
undercover in a refugee camp,
cocksure and unsure, signing my letters home
"Love, Morgan." It didn't stick. I chickened out.

But you held on, a truly self-made man
like Whitman, who turned Walter into Walt.
At parties in a row house you were renting,
you showed old movies on exposed brick walls,
threading the film, projecting black and white,
and you were Laurence Harvey, starring in
Room at the Top—ambitious, cool, and pushy,
but still the character we rooted for.
I think of you as the projectionist
who flashed a scintillating waterfall
of edginess, the hippest repartee.

Who else but Liam would gun himself down,
leaving a note that planned his funeral?
My grandfather killed himself with much less style,
no shotgun, just a bottle of rat poison.
You claimed that poets ought to kill themselves,
a starry, stormy, celebrated end,
but cancer and a heart attack convinced you.
I couldn't travel for the ceremony
but read about your handmade Italian shoes
arranged on steps in Saint Mark's in-the-Bowery
and how your friends could pick a pair and wear them,
keepsakes to keep you with them on their walks.

Thanks a lot, Liam. You transformed my life
by coaxing me to go in the dark, fly blind,
and take a chance on messing up my prospects.
Here is the letter I can never send
my rowdy, reckless, hip, foul-weather friend.

The Electric Guitarist

In memory of Jim Simmerman

"Ever the best of friends," your letters ended,
great expectations for a wave of years
that promised more reunions, correspondence.
But all that's over. The police were pleased:
you'd cleaned your room, and organized your papers,
and spread a plastic sheet on the bed you made
before you squeezed the trigger. Much less mess
than what a riot of pain your life had been:
arthritis that ruled out playing your Stratocaster,
bipolar riffs, binges of solitude
in bars, relationships blown to jagged bits,
and your dog, Bandit, dying before you did.

You were theatrical, always percolating,
"acting out" like a kid hopped up on conflict.
Your facial tic, compulsive blinking, betrayed
the turbulence within. You clashed with others,
but when I told you that you'd copped a line
of mine, you changed the ending of your poem.
I'm grateful that you talked your editor
into publishing my first book in his series
that barred (till my collection) all debuts.

Halfway from Provincetown to Arizona,
you stopped in Iowa City, meeting me
at Howard Johnson's by the interstate.
We visited the library to greet
our master's theses. You pulled out your volume,
ripped out the pages from the binding, and dropped
your poetry collection in the trash can,
returning the empty cover to the stacks.
"This one belongs to them," you said. "That's mine."

Executor

I talked to my father the day he died, if talk
is what you call it when the words are jumbled,
urgent as though imparting one last secret,
garbled on the cell phone. When I reached
the hospital and asked to see my father,
I waited for an administrator to meet me,
gazing at marble floor and coffered ceiling.
No, she told me, *it's hard for the families.*
I left but loitered in the blooming garden
and came back and demanded to view the body,
saying that I hadn't seen my father
in three years, had to see him now, before
they cremated him, and all I had was ashes.
Businesslike, but practiced in compassion,
she took me to the subbasement herself,
accompanied by an armed security guard.
Who knew how I'd react? I'd caused a fuss
already. Could go crazy, suicidal,
throw myself on the corpse, batter his face,
who knew? Down we went, silent, to a floor
hot as a sauna. I was sweating; they
were nervous. I looked at the holstered pistol.
Wrong floor. We had to go back up a flight.
Another corridor. They had me wait
until they could prepare my father's body.
They let me in, alone. The room was cold:
a big refrigerator door latched shut,
a gurney with a man tucked in, a sheet

up to his neck. His silver hair looked combed,
his eyelids slightly open. I could see
the sea green of his eyes, his lips apart
as if to resume the fevered gibberish
I couldn't translate, fatherly advice
I'd never learn to figure out on earth.
He would have been upset about his growth
of beard, the stubble he could not shave off.
I have to confess I sneaked a photograph
and kissed his forehead. It was cold, of course,
and hard as marble on a pumiced bust.
I stroked his hair. I wish I'd kissed his stubble.
Now he stays downstairs, his polished urn
committed to a British Airways bag,
a gesture to eternal transmigration,
and waits atop a filing cabinet
where I keep secrets, weighing down my life.

Daughter of a Preacher Man

The husband was a drunkard from Tow Law
in County Durham. Once a redcoat, what
did he do for a living? Drunkard. That's it.
The story doesn't say. Snow coming down,
thatched cottage growing cold, a cradle thrown
into the stone hearth's fire, but he had not
noticed the baby. The wife yanked her out,
grabbed her young son, walked through deep snow to town.

Mother and daughter died. The son survived
a childhood of inebriated weather,
worked as a donkey boy in a coal mine,
shunned liquor, crossed the ocean, and arrived
in Ohio, a seminarian, ordained:
my grandmother's quiet, dry, coldhearted father.

Recovering What's Lost

Nostalgia is the giddiest excursion
through plots of lilac, jasmine, honeysuckle.

You marvel over tick marks of erosion
in a creek bank, deep-gouged engraver's plate,

and lose yourself, abstracted by bamboo shadows
shimmery in the living room's late sunlight.

The other way of going back, however,
means opening the account books of a past

red-faced by debt, hysterical with fever
that won't break, desperation searing you.

Defeat restores, a generating force—
at least you hope so—burnishing the view:

a sheet of sunlight floating on the floor
like photographic paper in a bath.

Chaconne

I once heard a professor say
that any mystery that can be solved
    is not a mystery. The man
proposed a "God is dead" theology,
    based on Nietzsche, not the Bible,
and yet his most receptive audience
    was Baptist, congregants who "knew
their God had died." They writhed with him on the cross.

I'm listening to a sonata
composed by Jean-Marie Leclair, who served
    as violinist for a duke's court
but had to live in the outskirts of Paris
    in a shabby hovel by a tavern.
After a night of billiards, he was found
    in a pool of blood, stabbed in the back.
And that's a movie I would like to make.

Leclair's Chaconne in G minor plays,
obsessive violins examining clues
    in a ground bass. At the scene of the crime,
a gardener who discovers the composer
    becomes an automatic suspect.
And everything's a clue. As Thales says,
    "There are gods in all things." The click
of billiard balls, the caroms on green felt.

His curly wig's half off, powdered
and bloody. Through the doorway, his violin
     glows on the case's velvet lining.
He sprawls on cracked tiles of the vestibule
     of his cramped house with peeling stucco.
Horses are clopping on the cobbled street.
     Wagons are swaying. A crowd swarms.
Police are stumped. It's the eighteenth century.

     The gardener is detained, released.
A nephew looks suspicious, blames the uncle
     for his stalled musical career.
The widow has the usual motive: money
     she lacks, deserves, must scheme to get.
Anyone could stab a drunken man
     in his frock-coated back three times
and stop the air he's humming. Even his ghost

     would be no help. He couldn't see
his cowardly assailant pound the knife in.
     Flashbacks begin. He's making lace—
his father's craft—and tuning a violin,
     applying rosin to the bow
and stroking out a note, a scale, a run:
     a young musician married to
a dancer, dancing with her. Then she dies.

And then he meets his second wife,
a beautiful engraver named Louise.
        After his death, she carries on
her wifely duties, publishing his work
        and counting up the royalties.
Another flashback to a fiddlers' duel
        he fought with his rival, Locatelli.
Who won the concert? Who killed the violinist?

        The trick is that we never know,
and everyone's a suspect. We observe
        a scene from his only opera:
Circe the witch has cast a spell, transforming
        a nymph who's just a country girl
(although competing for a minor sea-god)
        into rock above a whirlpool—
love as the source of hate and homicide.

        All of them wanted him to die,
probably even Locatelli, all
        conspirators who act in concert.
Who struck the blows? One each for gardener,
        widow, and nephew, three in all?
The overture rejoices in a fugue
        where strings are stitching up the lace
of polyphonic clues. But nothing's solved.

V

The Lexicon of Things That Morph

Embarking

All of these years spent studying, late nights
cramming for exams, equipped you for this:
an evening at the harbor, the ship's lights
blinking awake, breeze blowing in the scent
of spices from a dockside factory.

When Venice was an empire of the sea,
her arsenal could produce a warship daily,
a fighting galley, oars sticking out of portholes
like the legs of a centipede crawling over waves.
Workers provisioned ships that glided past
windows along a canal, tossing coils
of rope and kegs of salted meat on board.

Instead of smashing champagne on a bow,
we ought to share a drink and toast good luck
to maiden voyages, as if, this time,
the *Titanic* might avoid the iceberg, arriving
to cheers in New York, gradually becoming
anonymous as passengers in steerage
who wait their turns to amble down the gangplank.

Sun dimming, foghorns bellow mating calls.
We think the ship's still docked, but as in dreams
we've slipped away already, toward the rocks
and ruined lighthouse by the harbor's mouth,
the sea beyond it merging into sky.

Living in Monterey

I can't believe how much I hitchhiked there—
which means, of course, I had to wait for rides,
and waiting was a privilege to bear
by the ocean at Point Piños. Riptides
made breakers scary. Sea lions basked on rocks
and barked into rough winds. Gulls glided. Cars
passed by, not slowing down to give me looks.
The sun retired, but I was given stars.

At night, I lay on the cold beach of Carmel.
I hitchhiked to Big Sur, stood on a bridge
below the redwoods, hearing a creek's trill,
picked up by a blue school bus, seats unlodged.

Instead of doing homework, I embraced
cool pastorals of the Pacific coast.

Cincinnati Haiku

After sequences by Etheridge Knight and Marilyn Chin

Once, I could order dim sum in Chinese. Now I stay home, sipping tea.

> Snow on Mount Storm, slopes
> at right angles. Sleds converge,
> sharp runners glinting.

Blocks of houses razed. Two stories remain: dark windows collecting stars.

> The car motor's off.
> Standing on the ferry deck,
> I'm frisked by the breeze.

Coal barge docked near trees. Catfish lurk in the river, but no one's fishing.

> Raking rocks, combing
> furrows in sand—Zen garden
> in a litter box.

Slice those ears off! a swimming instructor yells. *Your hands are razor blades!*

> Green-tiled house (its late
> owner killed in the front yard)
> gushes Christmas lights.

Violet sky through bare branches; full moon's whole note between open blinds.

> Harnesses, hard hats,
> chain saws, chipper—the tree crew
> pardons one white ash.

Parade on opening day—we stay home, turn off the Reds game, make love.

Autumn from a Passing Corolla

Red flecks erupt on ash-tree leaves
    like the flush on my lover's neck.
Don't starve these fevers. Gorge yourself!
    Soon enough, they will break.

Gaslight District

Why do I feel a pang of regret when I pass a particular lamppost
    on walks with my dog?

Why does it tilt toward the street, like a green candle that can't
    stay upright in a sconce?

Why does its silvery crown, a zigzag ring, tilt the opposite way,
    like a jaunty cap?

Why didn't I take a photo when vines rose up to the globe, the
    leafage a turtleneck sweater on a very long neck?

Why do embossed vines and leaves stick out like varicose veins on
    the green metal post?

Why did someone train real vines, now gone, to cover those
    artificial ramifications?

Why did homeowners, or gas-and-electric maintenance crews,
    chop the vines down to stubs?

Why did some caretaker plant a ring of stones around the circular
    garden that still holds the roots underground?

Why do I worry that vines, which I failed to identify, will never
    reemerge from the underworld of possibilities?

Why do some neighbors want all lampposts on our street to look
    alike, freshly painted, not flaking away autumnally?

Why does gaslight, flickering through its cloudy globe, give us a
    thumbs-up of fire?

Beginning with a Line from Turgenev's *On the Eve*

My God—the God of light and happiness—
eludes me, even though I love the light,
even though I revel in my wife.
Belief, though, fails to squeeze through the thin mesh
of transitory flashes on the gulf.
Twirling, interlocking lassos of light
vacillate on waves. One word, *goodbye*,
makes up the lexicon of things that morph.

What doesn't change? Even in rites of pleasure—
eating and drinking, hearing music, sex—
the sun's already set, red clouds remain
as residue, the tinge of coffee stain
in empty cups, erasure on erasure,
no deity required for wane or wax.

Crossing Guard

I finally get to join the safety patrol
and wear the webbed white belt and shiny badge,
but something's wrong. I wave a mob of school
kids from the curb, over the slippery edge

into a glittering canal. They swim
away, despite their clothes, with satchels for fins.
When other children rush to follow them,
I hold out my arms. But still they tumble in.

Later, sitting on the stone quay, I watch
the water rise toward levels the tides have marked—
algae, rust, and sludge—and then, like a lit match,
the waves flash with the last sunlight before dark

and an orange flotilla pushes into view.
Reaching down from a bridge, I catch a life vest,
still fat with air, and flip it to see who
migrates my way. Smooth as a marble bust,

a face beneath wet, matted hair looks hard
at me with a faint smile and bulging eyes.
I let it join the current. People crowd
the borders of the ditch and drop bouquets

that separate as they fall. Some blossoms float
among the bodies. Some land on drenched hair,
others on life vests: offerings of white
roses, delivered by barge. The lights that flared

scatter from the water as the parade
floats through, out to the darkening lagoon.
I should go too, but I watch the tide recede,
white flowers drifting by me, bunches of moons.

Ghazal of the Vaporetto

In memory of Norma and Yashdip

True Venetians sit behind glass, but I ride up front
on the waterbus, wind-bashed during my ride up front.

In the cabin, passengers hunch in fur coats and parkas,
reviewing the stock market reports. Why ride up front?

The black snake of the Grand Canal swallows us whole.
Wind smothers ambition with its scarf. To die, ride up front.

No wonder Wagner wrote *Tristan und Isolde* here.
The water pulls me with its lullaby: "Ride up front."

I look for chandeliers and reading lamps in the windows
of dark palaces. People who like to spy ride up front.

Wind pares away the encrustations of remorse.
"Lose yourself on the water," it sighs. "Ride up front."

Streets Full of Water

A college dormitory, dark, but morning
touches the window blinds like the gilt edges
of pages in books. A woman's getting up,
but all she sees are flashes from outside.
Everyone else is sleeping in, but she
is buttoning her shirt, grabbing her purse,
and slipping down the wide, high corridor
past dorm rooms and the stinky bunks of boys.
Her steps resound like drops of water falling,
and she unlocks a big door, opens it,
and there it is, the Grand Canal of Venice.

She's standing in a gondola, the only
passenger ferried to the other side.
She enters the Piazza, laughing, spinning
to see it in the round, and sauntering
past Florian's and the Basilica,
admiring pinkish diamonds, the Doge's Palace,
emerging on the quay where Black men sell
leather goods displayed on plain white sheets.
She doesn't need a purse, and she suspects
the Gucci would be counterfeit, a knockoff,
but she would like to find out who they are,
intrigued enough for coffee, but no more.

The tall men by the handbags look polite,
but one of them approaches, saying, "Miss,
I'm at your service, please," his accent British.
"I come from Senegal," he says and smiles.
"Is that what you would like to know of me?
Un peu de l'homme qui habite à *Venise?*"
Her gasp is audible, her laugh embarrassed.
He's like an actor who breaks through the screen
to reach a woman in the audience.
But then the Africans begin to flurry,
flapping like pigeons, bunching up their goods
in sheets and scattering. Police are coming.
"I'm sorry," he apologizes. "Find me."
The whole embankment empties, except for her.

Later that day, she finds him, and they share
a bistro table next to a canal
that looks pale green as jade and barely moves.
Tomorrow she is going to Saint George's.
Would he care to join her? Not that she
is so religious, really, but she likes
the local flavor of expatriates,
the plaques embedded in the church's walls
(there's one for Ruskin, one for Robert Browning),
and afterward they'll go to a trattoria.
That's the best part. "Oh, yes," he says, "of course."

***

And so the characters all come together
in the quaint church where English is the language:
Emily, who's studying abroad
in Casa Volta on the Grand Canal;
the merchant from Senegal who's selling handbags;
a painter who also plays the mandolin
(wearing silk breeches and a powdered wig
to play Vivaldi with an orchestra)
and lives here, runs a gallery in the Ghetto;
a self-professed "dumb plumber" and guitarist
who wants to find a job and stay in Venice;
his girlfriend who takes lessons from the painter
and sometimes models for his figure studies,
her hair extremely long, extremely black;
a would-be poet who would like to die
in Venice and be buried in San Michele,
where Ezra Pound and Joseph Brodsky rest;
a former rabbinical student who's lost his faith
and searches for what Henry James saw here,
his own "repository of consolations."

The plumber's studying Italian, trying
to get his break as an apprentice here,
though ancient pipes and nasty septic tanks
in squares where wells would be traditional
are hard to deal with, hardly picturesque,
but he's adept with wrenches, snaking pipes,
and plumbers are—good luck!—in short supply.

The painter's gone on tours of synagogues—
most of them hidden on the highest floors
of tenements, five windows that announce
where the five books of the Torah are observed—
to memorize the lush interiors
so he can sketch and paint what he recalls,
since photos are forbidden. He even owns
a yarmulke whose embroidery he designed.
He and the plumber bring their instruments
to Casa Volta, where they jam. The merchant
sings a Jacques Brel song, his bass voice booming.
They've congregated in the library,
starting to bond over Pinot Grigio.

Another day, the resident professor,
a randy novelist, lectures on how
aristocrats in silk rags begged on bridges
in Venice's last years as a republic,
decadent scene of gambling, masks, and sex.
Asked what he thinks, the African recites
a poem in French by Léopold Senghor,
letting them hear the "deep pulse of Africa."
Half con man, they suspect, and half chimera,
he whets their yen for anything exotic.
They call him their Othello, and he bows.
The would-be rabbi pushes up his glasses,
coughs for attention, shrugs, and asks them all,
"So what's my part? Shylock because I'm Jewish?"

***

All of them rent a speedboat and cruise out
on the lagoon, Emily navigating
with a big nautical map the wind roughs up.
The merchant from Senegal, standing at the wheel,
pilots the boat through channels, a labyrinth
that's treacherous for locals to explore.
They run aground, but he takes off his shirt,
leaps in the water, making others follow,
easing the boat off mudbanks in the shallows.

Back in the city, reeling after grappa,
the would-be poet wants to kill himself,
climbing the parapet of an arching bridge,
teetering, threatening to dive headfirst,
but ends in slapstick. Everyone gets drunker,
moving from wine bar to wine bar, but then
an accident intervenes—a chunk of marble
breaks from an ancient ledge and almost hits
the would-be poet walking near the wall.
They laugh, surrounding the crushed masonry.
Lights go on in windows. Heads peer out.
The explosion of the crash has woken up
the parish. Dogs are barking. Sleepers complain.

The little circle of expatriates
moves down the alley, next to a canal,
close to the building where the merchant lives.
But then a shadow moves, a figure bursts
from a doorway. The plumber pushes off
a sleeve that suddenly appears, pure reflex,

but then he notices a glint of metal
flashing, a blast, and then the painter crumbles.
Not brawlers, still they grapple with the gunman,
led by the merchant, pounding him and punching,
knocking his Magnum into the canal
and scrimmaging until they've pinned him down.

A member of a neofascist group
called Casa Pound—"the rest is dross"—has struck.
He wanted to eliminate the merchant,
just as he had ambushed Senegalese
compatriots and handbag sellers already.
He slipped inside and shot two as they napped,
waiting for more Black immigrants to kill.
The next day, Africans would march and shout
"Racists! Racists! Shame!" in the Piazza.

The group of temporary friends is stunned
and gathers in the painter's studio.
Since he's a little famous, locally—
a gallery has planned a one-man show
of watercolors, hidden synagogues—
authorities allow him to be buried
on San Michele. Emily's crushed and shaken.
The plumber's girlfriend turns out to have been
the mistress of the painter. Now she's calmed,
consoled by the merchant, potent as Othello,
mysterious and shrewd as Klee's *Black Prince*.
Quick sketches in her open notebook show
a passionate rebelliousness, a seething:
boys who lounge on a crumbling humpbacked bridge;
a woman in a kitchen, scaling fish.

The plumber's on his own but gets a job here,
repairing leaky faucets, clogged-up toilets.
The would-be poet needs to try his luck
at anything but verse. The Jewish man
has realized he'll never be a rabbi
but thinks he's closer to enlightenment.
Emily smiles, a little crookedly,
and asks him to have dinner at the casa.
Later, they'll go out on the balcony
and clamber up the balustrade to hop
to the roof of Peggy Guggenheim's museum,
sneaking like burglars to the sculpture garden.
Too dangerous? "We've done it as a prank.
Come on," she coaxes, "you've got to test the limits."

The merchant's busy wooing and seducing
the widowed mistress, putting his arm around her.
Although she doesn't look at him, she leans
her head against his shoulder and relaxes,
collaborating in their first embrace.
"I want to come back sailing my own yacht,"
he says, "and dock where I sold leather bags.
Mon cœur, let's go to Paris, where it's bright
at midnight and we'll stay up until dawn.
And you can paint. And I can make my fortune."
She acquiesces, gazes at his face.
Their kiss, reflected in a dark canal,
breaks up in flashes, flickering mosaics.

VI

The Teller's Cage

Gossip

The gossip of gray waves, along a stretch
of broken oyster shells, consoles the wretch
gazing upon the choppy Choptank. She
would love to merge in murky brine, to flee
the venom that's embossed on human speech.

Her marital secrets leak out in a screech
on party lines. Forbidden love can't teach
gospel to bigots who need her remedy:
                              the gossip of gray waves.

The woman, who's my mother, wants to reach
out of her kitchen window near a beach
in Florida, pluck an orange from a tree,
and squeeze it for fresh juice, and hear with glee
the breezes in royal palm fronds as they match
                              the gossip of gray waves.

Choosing a Reader

She's dead, and so she's hard of hearing, stuck
in a graveyard in Maryland. In fact,
she's ashes in a canister underground.
So first I have to drive six hundred miles,
arriving late at night, a harvest moon
orange on the river, park my car on gravel,
and dig until my garden trowel hits metal.
I'll need a Phillips screwdriver to open
the dirty urn. I'll need a spell, the best
special effects, to coax the bone and cinders
into a semblance of a human being.
"Son," she'll say, "why did you disturb me here?"
I know that what I show her must be worth
the trouble of her rising, as she clucks
her tongue at typos—getting her interested
for a short spell, to keep the pain at bay
while a lost world begins to materialize,
its radiance emerging from black letters.

Arguing about Computers

"It all comes down to one and zero, Mom,"
I said at breakfast, trying to explain
the mystery of computers. "I'm too old
for *that*," she said, "that shit." I tried to get
her interested in buying one herself,
thinking the binary system might excite her
since she had always liked to work with numbers.
"It's like Morse code," I said, "the dots and dashes."

My *yes* was answered by my mother's "No,
I hate computers. When the bank got theirs,
I couldn't be a teller anymore.
I had to quit. Computers took my job."
The miracle she craved, something to help
her keep on breathing, wasn't digital.
Stupidly, trying her patience, I persisted:
"It's like a light switch, Mom, on-off, on-off."

Library in a Dresser Drawer

My mother had a dirty mind.
I knew it from the paperback stash
she hid where it was hard to find.

Lust was the muse for whom I pined,
so I slid out the drawer of trash
my mother had. A dirty mind

is what we shared, but she had lined
the antique wood with dust and ash
protecting what was hard to find:

Jail Bait's the novel I reclined
with on her bed. Guilt whipped its lash,
my mother detecting my dirty mind.

But just as ducks mistake the blind,
her customers at the bank would have blushed
at what she hid. Instead, they'd find

a lady, proper and refined,
a teller with a drawer of cash:
my mom, who had a dirty mind
she hid to make it hard to find.

The Teller's Cage

My hands got dirty from the cash I handled,
working behind brass bars in a teller's cage.
And though it said "Head Teller" on my badge,
I couldn't get a raise. All my plans dwindled.

After I settled, when the bank closed, I bundled
worn, torn dollars with paper straps. On edge
for holdups, I never gave my alarm a nudge.
Mornings, I loved the crisp new bills I fondled.

Counting my cash, I often came up short.
Millions of dollars flowed, a tap opened up,
tinting me with a wash of currency.

The bank officials on the balcony
peered down, not sharp enough to see me slip
anything in my purse, my larcenous heart.

The Teller's Love Life

Abby was old enough to be my mother
so that's why, naturally enough, I thought
maybe she *was* my mother, not my sister.
She would have been eighteen when I was born,
not an adult, but easy to conceal
in a home for wayward girls in another state.

I was nine years old when Daddy killed himself
and Abby married, alone with a so-called mother
and Sarah, the middle sister who broke my nose,
pushing me upstairs to the attic. Visit
the sprawling house, and on the wooden stairs
my blood stains are still there. Mother took cruises,
and while she sipped her highballs in Bermuda
Sarah took care of me. Some joke! She had
the meanest eyes—oh, she was beautiful
but heartless—even her hands were mean, mean, mean.

The year I went to college, a finishing school
they forced me to attend, Abby was driving
Mother and Mrs. Stafford to the beach,
wearing sunglasses that obscured her view.
A Victor Lynn truck smashed into the car,
crushed Abby, killing her and Mrs. Stafford,
whose family sued and won. Mother was saved
by the suitcase she was holding on her lap,
but she was injured badly. I dropped out
to come back home and nurse her back to health.

They took what Abby left me in her will,
not just the money, which was bad enough,
but the huge Persian cat that we adored.
His name was Snooks. The picture in my locket,
even now, is Abby holding Snooks, bouffant
of gray fur, sweet expressions on both their faces.
But Sarah took it upon herself to take him
to the vet, have him put to sleep. She boasted,
"That was the happiest day of my whole life."
I can't help crying. Makes me so damned mad.

But I got back at her. She came to dinner,
one Thanksgiving, and when I served the turkey,
I asked her, "Sarah, does it meet your standards?"
"Why yes, indeed," she said, and so I said,
"I cooked it in the roasting pan we used
for Snooks's litter box." She stopped mid-bite,
spit out the morsel, got up, grabbed her husband,
and wouldn't even speak to me for a year.
It was well worth the silence. But we made up,
at least enough for civilized reunions,
and even spent our holidays together.
Blood is thicker, you know. She must have known
in her devil's heart that she had done me wrong,
ganging up on me, siding with Mother,
treating me like the orphan that I was.

Growing up in that house, haunted by death,
paying for room and board when I was twelve,
I felt like Cinderella, her evil stepsisters
rolled into Sarah. I didn't get a prince,

although I married, so I had to wait
year after year in a tiny Cape Cod cottage
built in the side yard of the monstrous house
that towered like a yacht above its dinghy,
until I met a glamorous soprano,
sweet as Abby, loving and vivacious,
an opera singer who stepped off the stage
to rescue me—a "pants role" she performed,
playing Siébel to Ezio Pinza's Faust,
outdoors at night, lions roaring, when the Met
spent summers at the Cincinnati Zoo—
so we could live, love, princesses together.

The Ruined Aristocrat

1. *All-Night Radio Call-In Show*

"Good evening, Mister Waters. I believe
the two of us may actually be related.
One of my ancestors named Edward Waters
came with the early colonists to Virginia,
but on the way they left him in Bermuda.
Some say he killed a man, but on the beach
he found some ambergris—you know what that is?"

Whale puke?

       "Throw-up. They use it for perfume.
He might as well have stumbled on pirate gold."

I love it! One more scoundrel in the family!
I do hope you're my cousin. What's your name?

"Miss Bobby is what all the neighbors call me."

How charming! Lost plantation decadence!
This call-in show must be the new Schwab's Drug Store
where I've found my latest movie character—
the ruined aristocrat in a row house!

"I paint, so I could paint the window screens,
like the sailboat I painted on my bathroom window
to keep the peeping toms from watching me."

Perfect! Yes, I can see those screen doors now—
Baltimore gallery of marble stoops,
perfect for an opening montage.

"My real name's something else. Friends call me Bobby
because my father hankered for a son,
fretted, afraid, since he was almost fifty
when I was born, he'd never have a boy
to be his heir, take over his dry goods store,
and so the nurse informed him, 'Little Bobby
is here!' And the name stuck."

                        How marvelous!
I'm giving you my private number. Call me.
I want to hear about our relative.

2. *The Ballad of Edward Waters*

In 1609, the fleet set sail
    for the Jamestown colony
but scattered when a hurricane
    raised mountains in the sea.

Through alps of waves and waterfalls
    of rain, the *Sea Venture* rose
to peaks then skidded down ravines,
    but soon the ocean's blows

knocked out the caulk between the boards
    and opened up the hull
so water entered, rising up,
    and soon the ship was full.

The admiral, Sir George Somers,
    pointed with his sword:
"Passengers and crew, start bailing.
    Throw cargo overboard."

Edward Waters, his right-hand man,
    stripped to his waist to drain
brine that rose from the leaky hull
    and down from the hurricane.

The whipstaff broke; wind ripped the sail
    and wound it around the mast.
Three days and nights, they pumped and prayed,
    exhausted from the blast.

Sir George caught sight of a flash of light
    that flitted close at hand,
a vision of Saint Elmo's fire,
    and then he shouted, "Land!"

The crew broke out the liquor, toasted
    Providence in their revels,
but the admiral scanned his charts and knew
    the place was the Isle of Devils,

which Spanish seamen called Bermuda,
    its archipelago
surrounded by a reef, renowned
    for sending ships below.

He feared the ship would run aground.
    The mate was sounding depths.
The vessel drifted on the reef
    and wedged within a cleft.

The coral could have ripped the hull,
    but all survived the wreck,
ferried ashore in boats they stored
    like turtles on the deck.

They landed on a pink-tinged beach
    by a turquoise lagoon,
surrounded by volcanic rocks
    and suddenly marooned.

The colonists found a paradise
　　but voted not to stay.
They rushed to build two pinnaces
　　to transport them away.

But Edward and Sir George explored
　　Bermuda's island chain,
rowing the ship's boat all around
　　the crescent-shaped lagoon,

taking measurements, drawing a map
　　and, on the waves, a whale.
Below the compass rose, it floated,
　　flipping up its tail.

With new ships built, they sailed again,
　　but the admiral returned
with Edward Waters to Bermuda.
　　Soon he would be mourned.

Some claim he died while chasing boars,
　　some from glutting on pork,
but dead he was, whatever the cause,
　　so the ship's crew set to work.

They buried his heart by a makeshift church,
　　shipped home the rest of the admiral,
tossing him into pickling brine
　　then stuffing him in a barrel.

The *Patience* left three men behind—
    Carter, Chard, and Waters—
who planted beans and pumpkins, built
    thatched cabins for their quarters,

and kept a watch for approaching ships
    from Bermuda's highest land,
and rowed their boat from isle to isle
    to walk along the strand.

Three kings, or three custodians,
    they searched for what the tide
washed in. Doubloons were scarce. They found
    no oysters with pearls inside.

But one day, as they walked along
    the shore of the lagoon,
they saw a wet, gray, distant heap—
    drowned body of a man.

Yet closer in, they realized
    they'd found their golden fleece
in a huge, waxy, sweet, and musky
    chunk of ambergris.

The trio's peace was broken. "Mine!"
    "No, mine!" "I saw it first!"
They wrestled on the beach. Tired out,
    they hauled it as they cursed,

heaving the load on board the boat
    and rowing through the sea.
They carried, lugged, grappled, and tugged
    the sperm whale's legacy.

Some say that Edward killed a man
    and hid in a limestone cave,
but that was a different castaway
    who bore the same last name.

These three compatriots could not
    agree who'd keep their riches
until they thought of how those caves
    made perfect hiding niches.

One morning, fishing in their boat,
    they traded fighting words,
punching and wrangling, swinging oars
    till all fell overboard.

One night, Chard yelled at Edward, "Choose
    your weapon, pistol or sword,"
but Carter hid the weapons until
    peace had been restored.

The best truce was the syndicate
    the three men finally came to,
planning to smuggle ambergris
    the Virginia Company laid claim to.

After two years had passed, a ship
  brought settlers and supplies.
They bribed the captain but were caught
  and forfeited their prize.

When Edward reached Virginia, he
  got married but nearly died
in the Powhatan massacre. Against
  a cypress both were tied

but loosened their ropes and found a boat
  on the bank of a nearby run.
They rowed back home. The following year
  they had their only son.

Edward Waters did not lament
  lost riches of ambergris:
a hiding place in his travel case
  guarded a hefty piece.

3. *If My Mother Had Dialed the Director's Private Number*

Miss Bobby phoned the talk show from the apartment
she shared with Carolyn, a singer who
gave lessons to pay for half of the monthly rent,
more economical for roommates, two
women alone, though no one else knew how,
decades ago, they'd traded wedding vows.

She loved to talk, but calling Mister Waters
shook her nerves. Research provided some relief,
though *Pink Flamingos* shocked the long-lost Daughter
of the American Revolution. She laughed
in spite of her aristocratic past
and had a hunch she'd fit right in the cast.

For manners made a personal disguise
Miss Bobby used while working in the bank.
When she said "queer," her tone said *it applies
to others, not myself*, and so she shrank
from calling her lover anything but "cousin."
Yet something rose in her and made her brazen

enough to phone the director. Stirred by Coke
and bourbon, she exuded so much charm
she found herself on set, and take by take
entered the movie business in the form
of bossy drama coach, daft socialite,
and tipsy housewife vacuuming at night.

Bit parts, but giving her safe harbor in
the port of Baltimore, in the Free State
where she could feel at home in her own skin
and publicize what's truly intimate,
joining a company where every role
clarified layers of her conflicted soul.

And took her back to a tropical vacation,
companion to a wealthy friend who napped
while she hung out on the sand with gay black men,
finally released from feeling trapped
by what was *proper*: lady who could breach
the social barriers on a steel-drum beach.

Production Notes for Imaginary Movies

"New Song of the South" on page 15: This poem proposes a way to remake Walt Disney's *Song of the South* (1946) so it acknowledges the African sources of the animated fables and represents the real experiences of African American slaves (as opposed to the racist and sentimentalized version of the live-action frame). Joel Chandler Harris set the Uncle Remus stories (published in 1880) during Reconstruction, but he actually heard and collected them in the midst of the Civil War while he worked on *The Countryman*, a newspaper produced at the Turnwold Plantation in Georgia. These folktales and many others appear in *The Annotated African American Folktales*, edited by Henry Louis Gates Jr. and Maria Tatar (Liveright, 2018).

"The Civil War Goes On" on page 31: This poem is based on notes I took while observing a reenactment of the Battle of Gettysburg in 1993. It also owes a debt to Tony Horwitz's *Confederates in the Attic* (Pantheon Books, 1998). I admire the films of Robert Altman, such as *Nashville*, and developed the scenario as if he had directed a raucous, freewheeling picture about reenactors.

"Patricia Keene" on page 47: The architects named in the first stanza of this imaginary movie (Frank Gehry, Peter Eisenman, Michael Graves, and Zaha Hadid) all designed buildings built in Cincinnati, the city where I live. I first saw the paintings of Jennifer Bartlett at an exhibition in the Walker Art Center in Minneapolis in 1984.

"Chaconne" on page 61: I began writing this imaginary movie after hearing Suzanne Bona, the host of *Sunday Baroque*, introduce a composition by Jean-Marie Leclair (1697–1764) by recounting the mysterious circumstances of his death. A chaconne is a musical form in which the composer develops variations on a theme above the constant repetition of a ground bass, as in Leclair's Chaconne in G minor, the sixth movement of "Deuxième récréation de musique" (Opus VIII). The professor mentioned in the opening stanza is Thomas J. J. Altizer, the author of *Living the Death of God*, who taught at Stony Brook University when I was an undergraduate.

"Streets Full of Water" on page 76: The title comes from a telegram sent by Robert Benchley after he arrived in Venice: "STREETS FULL OF WATER. PLEASE ADVISE." I developed this blank verse treatment because I wished Woody Allen would set a film entirely in the city, where part of *Everyone Says I Love You* (1996) takes place. The passage about "an actor who breaks through the screen / to reach a woman in the audience" alludes to a scene in *The Purple Rose of Cairo* (1985). Like Ezra Pound, another controversial artist, Allen has strong connections to Venice, where he married his wife Soon-Yi and where he performed with his jazz band at the Goldoni and Malibran theatres and, eventually, at La Fenice, for which he led fundraising efforts after a fire had gutted the opera house in 1996.

> Emily is the only character named in the poem, but here's the full cast of expatriates (all outsiders, standing apart even in their own communities):
>
> Emily Harrington: "studying abroad / in Casa Volta on the Grand Canal."
>
> Paul Durée: "the merchant from Senegal who's selling handbags." (His father Catholic, his mother Muslim, he's accepted by his fellow street vendors, all Muslim, but represents an outlier.)
>
> Walt Spiegel: "a former rabbinical student who's lost his faith."
>
> Roger Woods (also known as Ruggero Sylva): "a painter who also plays the mandolin / . . . and lives here, runs a gallery in the Ghetto."
>
> Joe Messick: "a self-professed 'dumb plumber' and guitarist / who wants to find a job and stay in Venice."
>
> Miranda Locke: "his girlfriend who takes lessons from the painter / and sometimes models for his figure studies."
>
> Galway Cooper (whose real first name is George): "a would-be poet who would like to die / in Venice and be buried in San Michele."
>
> Prof. Leonard (or Lenore) Brinkley: "the resident professor, / a randy novelist."
>
> Casa Volta is the alias I chose for Casa Artom, a house which serves

as the Venetian campus for Wake Forest University. It's located on the Grand Canal between Ca' Dario and the Peggy Guggenheim Museum. I visited the building during a research trip in September 1997, after meeting two students at a restaurant where the congregation of Saint George's, the Anglican church in Campo San Vio, dined after the service. I learned that the chaplain lived next door to Ezra Pound's house on Calle Querini and had a key; later that week his wife gave me a tour of its three floors, each with a single room. (An additional scene could show Emily, Walt, and Galway going on a tour of Pound's house.)

The parenthetical quotation after "a neofascist group / called Casa Pound" is part of the most famous passage in *The Cantos of Ezra Pound*: "What thou lovest well remains / the rest is dross" ("Canto LXXXI"). I'm making this allusion to suggest that fascism is "dross," the opposite of "What thou lovest well."

Donna Leon's *Blood from a Stone* begins with the murder of a Senegalese street vendor, referring to him by the derogatory term "*vu cumprà.*" At the end of the mystery, these *ambulanti* remain alien to Commissario Guido Brunetti and other Venetians. There's no realistic way to bridge the divide. In a movie, however, the impossible can happen, and people can make surprising connections.

The massacre of Senegalese street vendors actually took place in Florence on December 13, 2011, but I took the liberty of transferring the atrocity to Venice.

"The Ruined Aristocrat" on page 93: The first part is based on a conversation broadcast in the 1980s on Sally Jessy Raphael's radio show in Washington, DC. My mother phoned John Waters from the garden apartment she shared with her lover and secret wife, Carolyn Long, whom she had to call her "cousin" in order to rent a place together.

The second part is based on research about Edward Waters, the "scoundrel" who might be our common ancestor. I found three books especially useful:

William Strachey, *A true reportory of the wracke, and redemption of Sir THOMAS GATES Knight; upon, and from the Islands of the Bermudas: his coming to Virginia, and the estate of that Colonie then, and after, under the government of the Lord LA WARRE, July 15, 1610* (from *Purchas his Pilgrimes*, Vol. 4, Chap. VI., printed by William Stansby for Henrie Fetherstone "to be sold at his shop in Pauls Church-yard at the signe of the Rose" in London, 1625).

Captain John Smith, *The generall historie of Virginia, New England & the Summer Isles* (printed by I. D. and I. H. for Michael Sparkes in London, 1624).

Lorri Glover and Daniel Blake Smith, *The Shipwreck That Saved Jamestown: The* Sea Venture *Castaways and the Fate of America* (Henry Holt, 2008).

I also read William Barret's "A True Declaration of the Estate of the Colonie in Virginia" (Eliot's Court Press and William Stansby, 1610), R. Rich's "A Ballad of Virginia" (from *News from Virginia. The Lost Flocke Triumphant.* Edward Allde, 1610), and *Sea Venture: Shipwreck, Survival, and the Salvation of the First English Colony in the New World* by Kieran Doherty (St. Martin's Press, 2007), as well as a number of genealogical websites devoted to Edward Waters and his descendants, along with my mother's detailed account of our family history, preserved in a thick binder.

While working on drafts of the ballad, I thought of each stanza as a panel in the storyboard for a film. I tested my ballad stanzas by singing them to myself during the process of composition, using the centuries-old tune to "Sir Patrick Spens" (Child 58A) as sung *a cappella* by both Jean Redpath and Ewan MacColl.

The third part of the poem is a "what if" story based on my mother's worry that if she *did* call John Waters on his private phone number, he might want to cast her as a character in one of his films and recruit her into his stock company of Dreamlanders based in Baltimore.

A screenwriter adapting this poem for a prospective film might begin with a scene about the conversation on the radio call-in show and then move back and forth between Bermuda in 1609 and Baltimore in the 1980s.

John Philip Drury is the author of four previous books of poetry: *The Disappearing Town* and *Burning the Aspern Papers* (both from Miami University Press), *The Refugee Camp* (Turning Point Books), and most recently *Sea Level Rising* (Able Muse Press). He has also written *Creating Poetry* and *The Poetry Dictionary*, both from Writer's Digest Books. His awards include an Ingram Merrill Foundation fellowship, two Ohio Arts Council grants, and the Bernard F. Conners Prize from the *Paris Review*. He was born in Cambridge, Maryland, and grew up in Bethesda, raised by his mother and a former opera singer she called her cousin but secretly considered her wife. After dropping out of college and losing his draft deferment during the Vietnam War, he enlisted in the army and served undercover at the West German Refugee Camp near Nuremberg. He used benefits from the GI Bill to earn degrees from Stony Brook University, the Writing Seminars at Johns Hopkins, and the Iowa Writers' Workshop. After teaching at the University of Cincinnati for thirty-seven years, he is now an emeritus professor and lives with his wife, fellow poet LaWanda Walters, in a hundred-year-old house on the edge of a wooded ravine.

ALSO FROM ABLE MUSE PRESS

Jacob M. Appel, *The Cynic in Extremis: Poems*

William Baer, *Times Square and Other Stories; New Jersey Noir: A Novel;*
New Jersey Noir (Cape May): A Novel;
New Jersey Noir (Barnegat Light): A Novel

Lee Harlin Bahan, *A Year of Mourning: Sonnets: (Petrarch) Translation;*
Advent and Lent: Sestinas and Sonnets: (Petrarch) Translation

Melissa Balmain, *Walking in on People (Able Muse Book Award for Poetry)*

Ben Berman, *Strange Borderlands: Poems; Figuring in the Figure: Poems;*
Writing While Parenting: Essays

David Berman, *Progressions of the Mind: Poems*

Lorna Knowles Blake, *Green Hill (Able Muse Book Award for Poetry)*

Michael Cantor, *Life in the Second Circle: Poems*

Catherine Chandler, *Lines of Flight: Poems*

William Conelly, *Uncontested Grounds: Poems*

Maryann Corbett, *Credo for the Checkout Line in Winter: Poems;*
Street View: Poems; In Code: Poems

Will Cordeiro, *Trap Street (Able Muse Book Award for Poetry)*

Brian Culhane, *Remembering Lethe: Poems*

John Philip Drury, *Sea Level Rising: Poems*

Josh Dugat, *Great and Small: Poems*

Gregory Emilio, *Kitchen Apocrypha: Poems*

Rhina P. Espaillat, *And After All: Poems*

Anna M. Evans, *Under Dark Waters: Surviving the* Titanic*: Poems*

Nicole Caruso Garcia, *Oxblood: Poems*

Stephen Gibson, *Frida Kahlo in Fort Lauderdale: Poems*

Amy Glynn, *Romance Language (Able Muse Book Award for Poetry)*

D. R. Goodman, *Greed: A Confession: Poems*

Carrie Green, *Studies of Familiar Birds: Poems*

Margaret Ann Griffiths, *Grasshopper: The Poetry of M A Griffiths*

Janis Harrington, *How to Cut a Woman in Half: Poems*

Katie Hartsock, *Bed of Impatiens: Poems; Wolf Trees: Poems*

Elise Hempel, *Second Rain: Poems*

Jan D. Hodge, *Taking Shape: Carmina figurata;*
The Bard & Scheherazade Keep Company: Poems; Finesse: Verse and Anagram

Stephen Kampa, *World Too Loud to Hear: Poems*

Ellen Kaufman, *House Music: Poems; Double-Parked, with Tosca: Poems*

Len Krisak, *Say What You Will (Able Muse Book Award for Poetry)*

Emily Leithauser, *The Borrowed World (Able Muse Book Award for Poetry)*

Hailey Leithauser, *Saint Worm: Poems*

Carol Light, *Heaven from Steam: Poems*

Kate Light, *Character Shoes: Poems*

April Lindner, *This Bed Our Bodies Shaped: Poems*

David Livewell, *Pass and Stow: Poems*

Susan McLean, *Daylight Losing Time: Poems*

Martin McGovern, *Bad Fame: Poems*

Jeredith Merrin, *Cup: Poems*

Richard Moore, *Selected Poems; The Rule That Liberates: An Expanded Edition: Selected Essays*

Richard Newman, *All the Wasted Beauty of the World: Poems*

Alfred Nicol, *Animal Psalms: Poems*

Deirdre O'Connor, *The Cupped Field (Able Muse Book Award for Poetry)*

Frank Osen, *Virtue, Big as Sin (Able Muse Book Award for Poetry)*

Alexander Pepple (Editor), *Able Muse Anthology;*
   Able Muse: A Review of Poetry, Prose & Art (semiannual, winter 2010 on)

James Pollock, *Sailing to Babylon: Poems*

Aaron Poochigian, *The Cosmic Purr: Poems; Manhattanite (Able Muse Book Award for Poetry)*

Tatiana Forero Puerta, *Cleaning the Ghost Room: Poems*

Jennifer Reeser, *Indigenous: Poems; Strong Feather: Poems*

John Ridland, *Sir Gawain and the Green Knight (Anonymous): Translation;*
   Pearl (Anonymous): Translation

Kelly Rowe, *Rise above the River (Able Muse Book Award for Poetry)*

Stephen Scaer, *Pumpkin Chucking: Poems*

Hollis Seamon, *Corporeality: Stories*

Ed Shacklee, *The Blind Loon: A Bestiary*

Carrie Shipers, *Cause for Concern (Able Muse Book Award for Poetry)*

Gabriel Spera, *Twisted Pairs: Poems*

Matthew Buckley Smith, *Dirge for an Imaginary World (Able Muse Book Award for Poetry)*

Susan de Sola, *Frozen Charlotte: Poems*

Barbara Ellen Sorensen, *Compositions of the Dead Playing Flutes: Poems*

Rebecca Starks, *Time Is Always Now: Poems; Fetch, Muse: Poems*

Sally Thomas, *Motherland: Poems*

Paulette Demers Turco (Editor), *The Powow River Poets Anthology II*

Rosemerry Wahtola Trommer, *Naked for Tea: Poems*

Wendy Videlock, *Nevertheless: Poems; The Dark Gnu and Other Poems;*
   Slingshots and Love Plums: Poems; Wise to the West: Poems

Richard Wakefield, *A Vertical Mile: Poems; Terminal Park: Poems*

Gail White, *Asperity Street: Poems*

Chelsea Woodard, *Vellum: Poems*

Rob Wright, *Last Wishes: Poems*

www.ablemusepress.com

Printed in the USA
CPSIA information can be obtained
at www.ICGtesting.com
JSHW020851221023
50375JS00003B/109